THE JAR GARDEN

MAKING DELICIOUS SPROUTS
A HOW-TO BOOK FOR BOYS AND GIRLS

WRITTEN BY DOROTHY WEEKS, R.N., M.S.
ILLUSTRATED BY DON BERGGREN

2.50

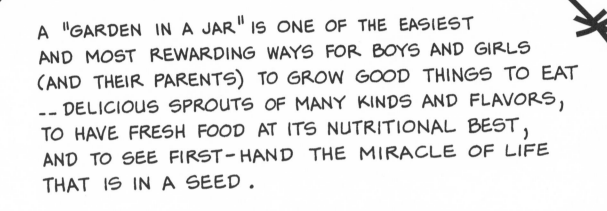

A "GARDEN IN A JAR" IS ONE OF THE EASIEST AND MOST REWARDING WAYS FOR BOYS AND GIRLS (AND THEIR PARENTS) TO GROW GOOD THINGS TO EAT -- DELICIOUS SPROUTS OF MANY KINDS AND FLAVORS, TO HAVE FRESH FOOD AT ITS NUTRITIONAL BEST, AND TO SEE FIRST-HAND THE MIRACLE OF LIFE THAT IS IN A SEED.

Published by
Woodbridge Press Publishing Company
Post Office Box 6189, Santa Barbara, California 93111

Copyright © 1976 by Dorothy Weeks and Don Berggren

World rights reserved.

Library of Congress Catalog Card Number: 76-428
International Standard Book Number: 0-912800-26-7

Published simultaneously in the United States and Canada

Printed in the United States of America

MARY, MARY, NEVER CONTRARY
HOW DOES YOUR GARDEN GROW ?

IT GROWS IN A JAR

IT GROWS IN A BIG OR LITTLE GLASS JAR;
YES, THAT IS THE EASIEST WAY BY FAR!
IT'S SO MUCH FUN AND SO EASY TO DO;
COME IN, JERRY, AND I WILL SHOW YOU, TOO.

HERE IS MY GARDEN FRESH AS CAN BE;
YOU SEE I HAVE QUITE A VARIETY.

THESE SPROUTS ARE SEEDS
  THAT JUST STARTED TO GROW;
THEY ARE JUST AT THEIR BEST—
  LIKE US, YOU KNOW.

SPROUTS ARE DELICIOUS
    IN SO MANY THINGS;

THEY MAKE SALADS AND SANDWICHES
        FIT FOR KINGS!

TO START MAKING SPROUTS,
   TAKE A ONE=QUART JAR
         I'M SURE YOU CAN FIND ONE
               WHEREVER YOU ARE.

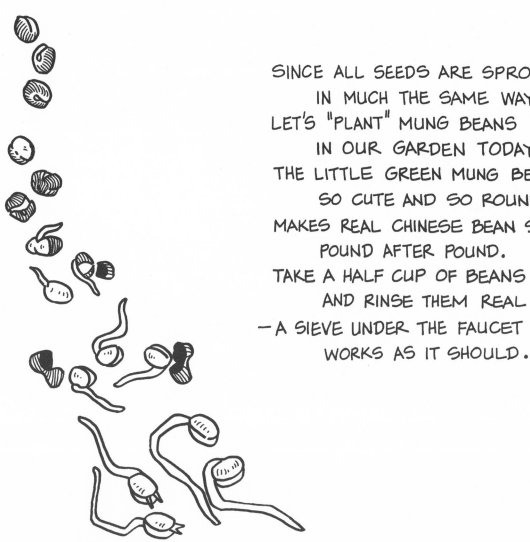

SINCE ALL SEEDS ARE SPROUTED
    IN MUCH THE SAME WAY
LET'S "PLANT" MUNG BEANS
    IN OUR GARDEN TODAY.
THE LITTLE GREEN MUNG BEAN,
    SO CUTE AND SO ROUND,
MAKES REAL CHINESE BEAN SPROUTS,
    POUND AFTER POUND.
TAKE A HALF CUP OF BEANS
    AND RINSE THEM REAL GOOD.
—A SIEVE UNDER THE FAUCET
    WORKS AS IT SHOULD.

WE PUT IN THE RINSED BEANS —
    SEE HERE THEY ARE.
THEN WE ADD WATER
    HALF WAY UP THE JAR.
FROM EIGHT TO TWELVE HOURS
    WE SOAK OUR SEEDS
IN FOUR PARTS OF WATER
    TO ONE OF SEEDS.

ITS EVENING—
      WE'RE POURING THE WATER OUT.
IT'S FUN TO TURN OUR BOTTLE ABOUT,
AND POUR FROM A TOP WITH HOLES, NOT A SPOUT.

OUR SEEDS ARE NOW FAT
AND READY TO SPROUT.

A LITTLE SHAKE OF THE JAR
WHEN THE WATER IS OUT
PUTS YOUR BEANS ON THE SIDE
WHERE THEY CAN SPROUT.

19

SEEDS LIKE TO SPROUT
 WHERE ITS WARM NOT TOO BRIGHT—
  IN A COZY CUPBOARD THEY ARE JUST RIGHT.
   THEY WILL ALSO SPROUT ON A COUNTER TOP
    WHERE YOU CAN WATCH THEM GROW
     WITHOUT A STOP.

IT'S NITE—WHILE WE SLEEP
    IN OUR COZY BEDS
SOMETHING WILL POP
    IN OUR LITTLE BEANS' HEADS.

IT'S MORNING AGAIN —
WE CAN HARDLY WAIT...

...TO PEEK AT OUR SEEDS.
YES, THEY'RE ALL FIRST RATE!
THEY'VE BURST OPEN THEIR COATS —
THEY DIDN'T FAIL!
WE CAN SEE CRACKS OF WHITE —
MAYBE A TINY TAIL.

WE'LL TURN THE WATER ON
HERE AT THE SINK —
WHAT AN EASY WAY
TO GIVE SEEDS A DRINK !
GARDENS NEED PLENTY
OF NICE, GENTLE RAIN ;
WE'LL RINSE TWICE A DAY
SO THEY WONT COMPLAIN.

UPSIDE DOWN AGAIN —
   THE WATER POURS OUT.
A WEE SHAKE
   AND BACK ON THEIR SIDES
      TO SPROUT.

IN THREE TO FIVE DAYS
   PUT YOUR JAR IN THE SUN ;
     YES, RIGHT IN THE WINDOW
       AND WATCH MAGIC COME !
        SEE, IT'S TURNING A MUCH RICHER,
       DARKER GREEN ;
         IN THREE HOURS OUR SPROUTS
           WILL BE FIT FOR A QUEEN !

31

OUR SPROUTS WERE YUMMY BUT WE HAVE SOME LEFT.
WE WANT TO SAVE THEM AT THEIR VERY BEST.
WE'LL PUT A LID ON OUR JAR GARDEN — CLOSE IT, AIRTIGHT —
IN THE REFRIGERATOR IT WILL KEEP JUST RIGHT.
(STORED SPROUTS RAISE IN VALUE SEVERAL DAYS LONG
BUT AFTER A WEEK THEY SHOULD ALL BE GONE .)
START SPROUTING AGAIN
BEFORE YOUR SPROUTS ARE ALL GONE
YOU WILL BE SURPRISED
THAT IT WON'T TAKE VERY LONG .

NEXT TIME WE PLANT, JERRY, WHAT SHALL IT BE ?
IN SEEDS THERE IS SUCH A VARIETY.

THERE'S CRISP ALFALFA —
FOR US, NOT A COW!
IN SALADS AND SANDWICHES
THESE SPROUTS ARE A WOW!

THE ROUND, FLAT LENTILS
ARE ALSO REAL GOOD
IN FRESH, CRISP SALADS
WITH OTHER RAW FOOD.

RADISH AND ALFALFA,
SPROUTED TOGETHER,
ARE SO YUMMY
WE COULD MUNCH THEM
FOREVER.

BUCKWHEAT AND PEA SPROUTS
ARE TWO OF THE BEST ;
CRISP, SWEET, AND JUICY —
YOU'LL EAT THEM WITH ZEST !

PEA SPROUTS

BUCKWHEAT SPROUTS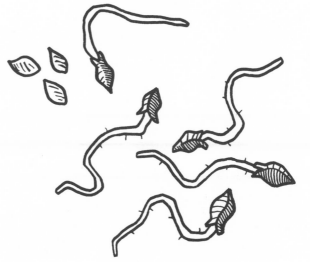

IT IS HARD TO COUNT ALL THE MANY KINDS
OF SEEDS YOU CAN SPROUT —
IT CAN BLOW YOUR MIND !

DID YOU KNOW,
   IN OUR JAR GARDEN
      NO ONE NEEDS
         TO SPEND PRECIOUS PLAYTIME
            PULLING PESKY WEEDS!

SEEDS SPROUT IN PLANES, BOATS, AND DEEP DOWN IN HOLES...

...THEY EVEN SPROUT FINE
    ON TOP OF FLAG POLES.

MOM'S FRIEND SPROUTS SEEDS
IN HER OFFICE DESK DRAWER
HER BOSS FOUND IT OUT —
NOW SHE SPROUTS ALL THE MORE!

DAD HAS A FRIEND
WHO SPROUTS IN A SACK,
WHILE HE CLIMBS TALL MOUNTAINS —
PACK ON HIS BACK.

WE ALWAYS GROW SPROUTS
ON OUR TRIPS IN THE CAR,
SO WE HAVE OUR FRESH FOOD
WHEREVER WE ARE.

(WE HAVE YET TO SEE KIDS
   REFUSE TO EAT
      THE SPROUTS THEY HAVE GROWN —
         THEY THINK THEY'RE REAL NEAT !)
            HERE ARE A FEW VERY GOOD REASONS WHY
               SPROUTING OUR FOOD
                  IS THE VERY BEST BUY.

NUTRITION
VALUE
PROTEIN
HEALTHFUL

AND THERE'S TWICE THE PROTEIN
IN FOOD EATEN RAW.
(A REAL FOOD EXPERT
TOLD THAT TO OUR MA.)

JUST ONE RADISH SPROUT
  WITH TWO TINY, GREEN LEAVES
    HAS THE FOOD OF A WHOLE ONE,
      IF YOU PLEASE.

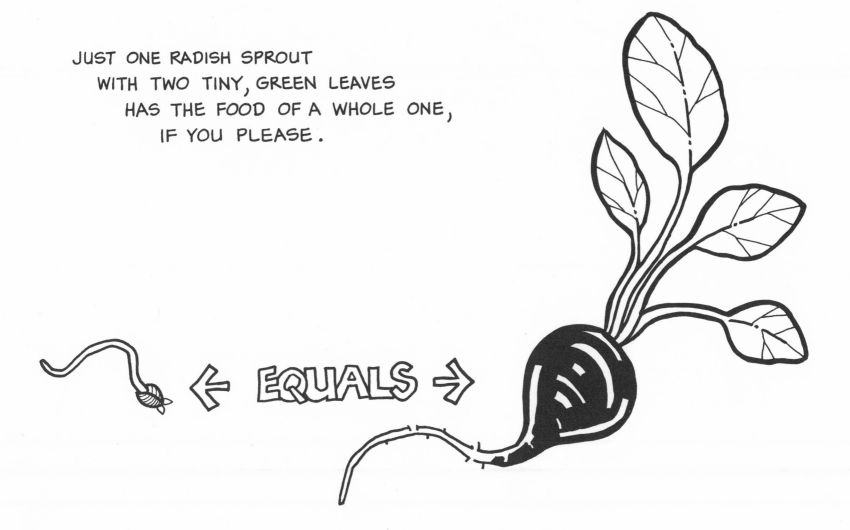

ANOTHER GOOD REASON FOR LEARNING TO SPROUT—
IT HELPS US TO SEE WHAT OUR LIFE'S ALL ABOUT.
WHILE WE HELP OUR SEEDS GROW,
WE ARE GROWING TOO.
IT MAKES US RESPONSIBLE,
ISN'T THAT TRUE?

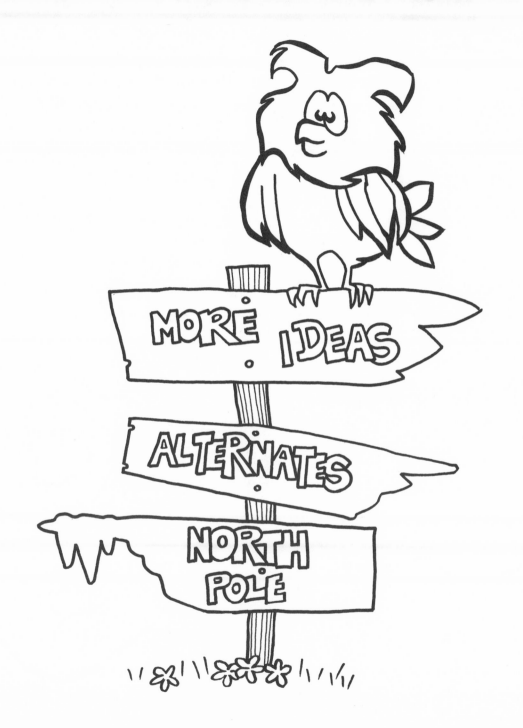

SOME TIPS FOR PARENTS AND BOYS AND GIRLS

ON HOW TO MAKE GOOD SPROUTS

1. SPROUTS LIKE TO BE KEPT DAMP BUT NEVER SITTING IN WATER.

2. SPROUTS LIKE TO BE KEPT WARM, FREE FROM DRAFTS, AND DIRECT HEAT OR SUNLIGHT. BETWEEN 75-85°... PERFECT !

3. SPROUTS LIKE TO BE RINSED AT LEAST EVERY MORNING AND EVENING. LARGE BEANS, PEAS, OR SOYBEANS LIKE AN EXTRA RINSE IN THE MIDDLE OF THE DAY.

4. SPROUTS LIKE LOTS OF ROOM TO BREATHE. EVEN WHEN SPROUTS ARE ALMOST LARGE ENOUGH TO EAT, AT LEAST A THIRD OF YOUR JAR SHOULD BE EMPTY TO ALLOW AIR TO CIRCULATE.

5. TO ADD CHLOROPHYLL TO YOUR SPROUTS, LETTING THEM "GREEN UP" A LITTLE, PLACE YOUR JAR IN A WINDOW TO GET SUNLIGHT FOR THREE TO TWELVE HOURS BEFORE EATING THE SPROUTS. CHLOROPHYLL IS A BLOOD BUILDER AND AN AID TO DIGESTION AND ASSIMILATION OF FOOD. IT HELPS BOYS AND GIRLS TO GROW.

NOTE: SOME COMMERCIAL BEANSPROUTS ARE BLEACHED TO REMOVE ALL TRACES OF CHLOROPHYLL. WHAT A PITY!

HELPFUL HINTS

<u>EQUIPMENT — JARS AND LIDS</u> : THERE ARE MANY SUCCESSFUL SPROUTING METHODS. THE JAR GARDEN WAS CHOSEN BECAUSE AFTER THIRTY YEARS OF EXPERIMENTING IT IS STILL MY FAVORITE. AND EVERYONE CAN GET A JAR. JARS EQUIPPED FOR SPROUTING MAY BE PURCHASED AT YOUR HEALTH FOOD STORES. IF YOU CAN'T FIND THESE, ANY WIDE-MOUTH JAR WORKS FINE — WITH A PIECE OF NYLON STOCKING AS A COVERING. THE STOCKING MATERIAL CAN BE SECURED TIGHTLY TO THE TOP OF THE JAR WITH A RUBBER BAND.

<u>SEEDS</u> : GET THE FINEST SEEDS AVAILABLE AT YOUR MARKET OR HEALTH FOOD STORE. I HAVE MADE EXCELLENT SPROUTS WITH SEEDS AND BEANS FROM THE LOCAL MARKET. HOWEVER, I RECOMMEND ORGANICALLY GROWN SEEDS. SEEDS THAT HAVE BEEN CHEMICALLY TREATED FOR PLANTING SHOULD NOT BE USED.

<u>WATER</u> : THE WATER THE SEEDS ARE SOAKED IN BEFORE SPROUTING SHOULD BE AS PURE AS POSSIBLE. RECENTLY, I HAVE USED BOTTLED SPRING WATER TO SOAK MY SEEDS. AFTER SOAKING, THIS DRAINED-OFF VITAMIN-AND MINERAL — PACKED WATER IS FINE FOR DRINKING, COOLING ——OR EVEN FOR WATERING YOUR FAVORITE HOUSE PLANTS.

WHEN TO "HARVEST" YOUR SPROUTS

LENTILS........ WHEN SHOOT IS ABOUT AS LONG
AS THE LENTIL IS WIDE.

ALFALFA....... WHEN SHOOT IS 1 TO 2 INCHES LONG.
THIS WILL BE ABOUT THE TIME THE
FIRST LEAVES APPEAR.

LARGE BEANS.. ¼ TO ½ INCH LONG – ABOUT TWO DAYS.

MUNG BEANS.. ANY TIME AFTER SHOOT FIRST APPEARS
UNTIL IT IS FOUR INCHES LONG.
READY IN THREE DAYS.

PEAS......... ¼ TO ½ INCH LONG. SHOOT ABOUT AS
LONG AS THE PEA IS WIDE.

RADISH........ ½ TO 1 INCH. LONG.

SOY BEAN.... ¼ TO 1½ INCH LONG.

OTHER GOOD REASONS FOR SPROUTING

1. SPROUTS ARE A NATURALLY NUTRITIOUS FOOD – COMPLETELY UNPROCESSED, UNREFINED, UNSPRAYED –– NATURALLY GOOD!

2. SPROUTS MANUFACTURE A RICH SUPPLY OF PROTEINS, MINERALS, VITAMINS, AND OILS. THEY CAN BE CLASSIFIED AS A COMPLETE FOOD. THEY ARE AS RICH IN PROTEIN AS MEAT AND AS HIGH IN VITAMIN C AS CITRUS FRUITS.

3. SPROUTS ARE VERY ECONOMICAL. ONE POUND OF SEED WILL PRODUCE EIGHT OR NINE POUNDS OF "HARVESTED" FOOD. THE MOST NUTRITIOUS OF ALL SPROUTS – THE SOYBEAN – COSTS JUST A FEW PENNIES FOR A LARGE SERVING.

4. SPROUTS ARE A BOON FOR DIETERS. NOWHERE CAN YOU GET MORE NUTRITION WITH FEWER CALORIES.